"FAMILY," HE SAYS! WOULD THAT I WAS!

FOR NONE LOVES HIS FAMILY MORE THAN YOU, JOB!

ELIPHAZ. A TEMANITE, FROM TEMAN, A PLACE KNOWN FOR ITS WISDOM.

YES, A MAN WHO LOVES HIS FAMILY, BUT ALSO A LOVER OF WISDOM!

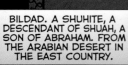

BILDAD. A SHUHITE, A DESCENDANT OF SHUAH, A SON OF ABRAHAM. FROM THE ARABIAN DESERT IN THE EAST COUNTRY.

JOB! I DON'T KNOW WHAT YOU DID TO DESERVE THIS WEALTH AND FAMILY--

--BUT, LET ME KNOW SO I CAN DO IT, TOO!

ZOPHAR. A NAAMATHITE, FROM THE TOWN OF NAAMAH ON THE BORDER.

TO JOB. A GENEROUS, FAITHFUL, AND GODLY MAN!

IT'S A GOOD THING HE IS HUMBLE, OR ALL THIS PRAISE WOULD GO TO HIS HEAD!

ELIHU, THE BUZITE. THE YOUNGEST OF JOB'S CLOSE CIRCLE OF FRIENDS. HIS NAME MEANS "MY GOD IS HE".

EARLY THE NEXT MORNING.

JOB DID AS HE SAID.

AS HE ALWAYS DID.

I COME TO YOU, MY LORD, ON BEHALF OF MY CHILDREN.

YOU HAVE BLESSED ME WITH THEM--

--IF THEY HAVE CURSED YOU IN THEIR HEARTS, ACCEPT THIS OFFERING!

JOB KNEW GOD OBSERVED HIS ACTIONS.

BUT HE WAS UNAWARE THAT SOMEONE--SOMETHING--ELSE OBSERVED HIM AS WELL.

JOB 1:5

IN THE HEAVENS, THE SONS OF GOD PRESENTED THEMSELVES BEFORE THE LORD.

AND ANOTHER-- THAT UNSEEN OBSERVER--CAME AMONG THEM AS WELL.

A FALLEN ONE.

THE FIRST OF THE FALLEN.

SATAN.

JOB 1:6-7

IN JOB'S FIELDS.

C'MON, OL' GIRL--

WHAT WAS THAT?

THUMP THUMP

RUN!!!

THE HOME OF JOB'S ELDEST SON, OMAR.

DID YOU REST WELL, COL?

YES, BUT NO THANKS TO YOU GUYS, DAVINIA!

HOW LONG DID JETH PLAY HIS LUTE AFTER I WENT TO BED?

TOO LONG, COL! TOO LONG!

LET'S FIND SOME FOOD.

MY HUSBAND IS STILL SLEEPING, BUT HE'S ALWAYS HUNGRY WHEN HE FIRST WAKES UP.

THERE'S PLENTY LEFT! OMAR AND THE OTHER BOYS ARE STILL AWAKE!

DO YOU HEAR SOMETHING?

I'VE NEVER SEEN...

IT'S...IT'S...IT'S COMING RIGHT AT US!!!

LET'S GET OUT OF HERE!

WHERE CAN WE GO?

JOB 1:20

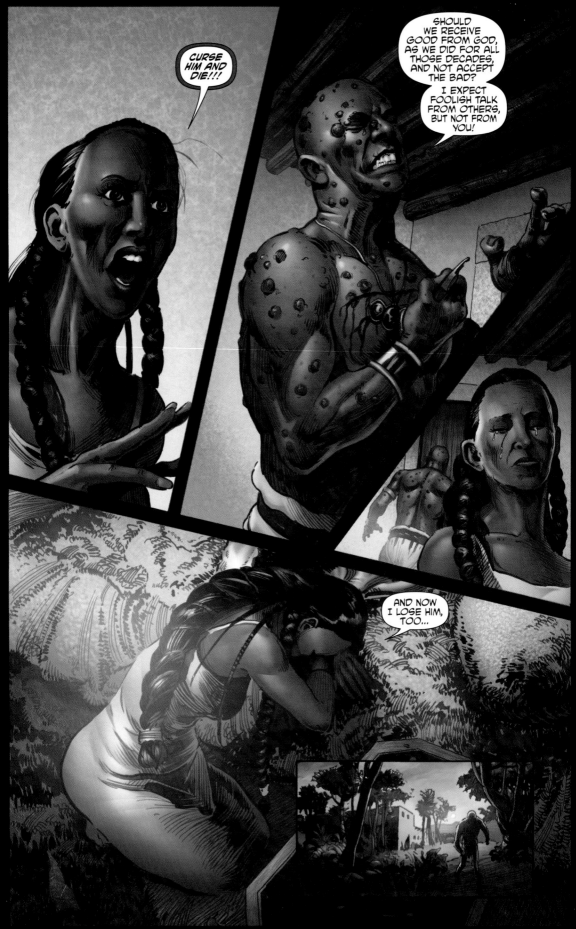

JOB 2:8

JOB 13:20-17:16

JOB 31:1-32:22

JOB 36-37

JOB 42:3-42:7

JOB 42:9

JOB'S FRIENDS DID AS THE LORD TOLD THEM.

AND JOB, TOO, DID AS THE LORD TOLD HIM.

LORD, MY FRIENDS COME BEFORE YOU WITH THIS OFFERING!

THEY RECOGNIZE AND REPENT OF THEIR SINS!

THEY OFFER THIS SACRIFICE AS PAYMENT FOR THEIR SINS AGAINST YOU!

AND THE LORD DID AS HE PROMISED.

JOB 42:9

JOB 42:9

THE BOOK OF JOB

The author of the book of Job is not known. Bible scholars think the four most likely candidates are Job, Elihu, Moses or Solomon. Because Job seemed to know about Adam and the Noahic flood it appears these events happened sometime after the Tower of Babel. Job is included in the Wisdom Books of the Old Testament, thus named because they help us to see life's circumstances from God's perspective.

From the book of Job we learn that Satan can only bring financial and physical destruction on us if he has God's permission. God alone has power over what Satan can, or cannot do. The book is very clear that we cannot understand the "whys" behind the great suffering in the world but we can see that suffering is sometimes allowed to purify and strengthen our soul. In all of life's circumstances God is enough and is deserving of all of our praise and loyalty.

After a scene in Heaven where Satan accuses Job, God grants permission, within certain boundaries, for suffering to come to Job. After Job loses his family, his wealth and his health, three of his friends come to "comfort" him, but they insist his suffering is punishment for sin in his life. Job, however, remains devoted to God through all of this and contends that his life has not been one of sin. A fourth man tells Job to humble himself and submit to God's use of trials to purify his life. Finally, Job questions God Himself and learns valuable lessons about the sovereignty of God and his need to totally trust in the Lord.

The Book of Job asks three questions that are answered in the Lord Jesus Christ. The first question is, "*Who can bring what is pure from the impure? No one!*" Jesus has paid the penalty for our sin and has exchanged it for His righteousness, thereby making us acceptable in God's sight (Hebrews 10:14).

Job's second question, "*But man dies and lies prostrate; Man expires, and where is he?*"
This question about eternity is answered only in Christ. With Christ, the answer is eternal life in Heaven. Without Christ, the answer is an eternity in "outer darkness" where there is "weeping and gnashing of teeth" (Matthew 25:30).

Job's third question is, "*If a man dies, will he live again?*" We do indeed live again if we are in Christ. 'Death has been swallowed up in victory.' 'Where, O death, is your victory? Where, O death, is your sting?'" (1 Corinthians 15:54-55).

The Book of Job reminds us that there is a cosmic conflict going on behind the scenes that we usually do not know about. Often we wonder why God allows something, and we question or doubt God's goodness without seeing the full picture. The Book of Job teaches us to trust God under all circumstances.